*Rock and f?, graves, and hope — the coming of the Irish to CANADA.*

## Apples on the Nashwaak

*Thanks for everything, Kin...*

*I hope you enjoy the read.*

*Sept. 2023*

# Apples on the Nashwaak

## Neil Sampson

Chapel Street Editions

Copyright © 2019 by Neil Sampson

All rights reserved

Published by
Chapel Street Editions
150 Chapel Street
Woodstock, New Brunswick E7M 1H4
www.chapelstreeteditions.com

ISBN 978-1-988299-25-9

**Library and Archives Canada Cataloguing in Publication**
Title: Apples on the Nashwaak / Neil Sampson.
Names: Sampson, Neil, 1952- author.
Description: A poem.
Identifiers: Canadiana 20190168080 | ISBN 9781988299259 (softcover)
Classification: LCC PS8637.A53854 A77 2019 | DDC C811/.6—dc23

Book design by Brendan Helmuth

Printed in Canada

**Dedication**

For all who've been told it's too late.

"... let me go, that I may hide myself in the field ..."

                                            1 Samuel 20:5

# Contents

Foreword . . . . . . . . . . . . . . . . . . . . . . . . . .i

Preface. . . . . . . . . . . . . . . . . . . . . . . . . . . v

Apples on the Nashwaak 2017 . . . . . . . . . . . . . . . 1

1878 – 1896 Bucksaw and Plough. . . . . . . . . . . . . . 5

1897 – 1902 The brave, to the New Land . . . . . . . . . .13

1897 – 1902 …the tortured, to follow . . . . . . . . . . .23

1903 – 1905 Flowers and Whispers. . . . . . . . . . . . . .33

1906 – 1939 Under the sun . . . . . . . . . . . . . . . . .43

1940 – 1952 The weight of a straw . . . . . . . . . . . . .51

1952 – 2017 The loss of full circle . . . . . . . . . . . .61

Acknowledgements . . . . . . . . . . . . . . . . . . . . .83

About the Author . . . . . . . . . . . . . . . . . . . . .85

# Foreword

Neil Sampson's first book, *Apples on the Nashwaak*, with its emphasis on time and place combined with dramatic action, fits neatly into the long tradition of storytelling in poetic form. In it, the poet-narrator relates the history of Irish settlement in Central New Brunswick. He begins in the present with an opening line that will resonate throughout the book:

"Only four trees are still alive. / The last of that first / generation …"

These words introduce some of the narrative's major themes: survivors, existence, the challenges of establishing and continuing a settlement in an untamed, natural world, and the omnipresence of death.

The narrative is then ordered chronologically from 1878 to 1952 and, at the end, back to the present. It tells the story of Michael Maguire's arrival, "out of Ireland: Enniskillen, / County of Fermanagh." It narrates the sea voyage from Ireland and the arrival in the New Land, with all the hardships and difficulties associated with tree clearing and home building in the wilderness. It ends with the twin themes of survival and memory: "Children / hugging the chimney, / warm long after / the embers had died."

Snippets of individual stories thrive alongside the broader picture of the way in which world events touch upon the characters' lives as the narrative moves through the first half of the 20th century. The last section sees a return to the poem's starting point and the reappearance of the first-person narrator who summarizes both the older memories and the contemporary scene.

The poem also returns to those first four trees, survivors all. Yet death will come to this land, to those trees, to those four pioneers "cankered with rot; / bark skinned, limbs / thin, draped in swags / of moss." "They've come / to where they can die." "And I've come to where / I can let them go." Indeed, the narrative sequence has come full circle.

While it is easy to sketch the story, it is much more difficult to describe the richness of each metaphor, the power of each carefully weighed word, the strength of each line division, and the shock that arises from the juxtaposition of contrasting words and scenes. In addition, the frequent repetitions remind us of seasonal flowers and plants, born from the land and plucked like ripe fruit from laden autumn branches.

The poet-narrator also uses the epistolary mode to great effect. The letter from Millie to Daniel is a fine example of letter writing, as is Hanna's letter to Shannon. Effective, too, is the poet-narrator's use of dialogue. Both these devices enable the reader to see deep into the characters and follow the workings of their hearts and minds. That said, actions speak louder than words, and the characters are all summarized in what they are seen to do.

Neil Sampson has lived this poetry sequence, worked this land, dirtied his hands with its soil, enriched his mind and his soul with its sadness. Antonio Machado once wrote of a *landscape so sad that it possesses a soul (paisaje tan triste que tiene alma)*. The Nashwaak of Neil Sampson also has a soul, a power and a possessiveness that grows up from the rock and sweeps through the soil to grasp the reader's attention. It's not surprising that the manuscript of *Apples on the Nashwaak* was given the Writers' Federation of New Brunswick 2018 Alfred G. Bailey Award for poetry.

This is poetry of the best kind, rooted in the landscape, climbing skyward, like a fruiting apple tree or a flowering vine, then returning to the soil, to lie there, battered and bruised, anticipating the arrival of the reader, waiting for the opportunity to take root and flourish in that reader's heart.

Roger Moore<br>
Professor Emeritus<br>
St. Thomas University

# Preface

I live in the woods.

Off the corner of our lot, a gravel road climbs to a fifty-acre field, to where blankets of paintbrush blend into sky. The Nashwaak River Valley runs far below.

The field lies deserted now, abandoned to wild roses and raspberries. Rock piles — 150-year heaps — half submerged in the treeline, icebergs of the understorey.

A meadow carved from the forest, a straggle of old apple trees, a lilac at the corner of a stone foundation: all that's left of a life long gone.

This was a homestead once: house, barn, paddocks and sheds; gardens behind fences of cedar rail and stone. The pioneers' existence: held in the balance of rain cloud and sun, in what could be squeezed from the earth — one season's bounty removed from death.

But there were blessings here too, for those who would look. Adults rarely did — minds preoccupied: understandably so. But they missed the gifts in the simple things, in what the children saw: batches of piglets and newborn calves; haymows with kittens; bounding lambs on new green; sunset's orange on the aspen grove; dandelion chin-bouquets.

I come here to run my dogs. They love to explore, to sniff every point on the compass. An open door to the wild, it stirs the wolf in their blood.

But not to dogs only are these latitudes infectious. A cross-species transmission occurs, a spillover into imagination. Thoughts, scattered at first, soon gather to lines and themes, precipitate into stories.

This field, these woodland trails still framed through a thousand square miles of forest — walk them; go deep. Though feet lose their way, the mind finds the path to a settled place. The soul inhales, quiets, soars; begins to nestle in.

*Apples on the Nashwaak* tells the stories of five generations of Irish families who called this place home. And while actual events are referenced and form the bases for some of the storylines, what follows is free flow, a river on the run. Facts carried, facts buried — trails of truth through a field of fiction.

Neil Sampson<br>
Durham Bridge, New Brunswick<br>
2019

# Apples on the Nashwaak
2017

Only four trees are still alive.
The last of that first
generation
ponder existence and being
unable to walk
— no chance of pilgrimage —
have seeded their hope of redemption
in Self.
They point to their wounds.
Canopies —
 thin upper spheres now shrunken by half;
 meagre fruit —
 scratch for sky
 and boast
 *We're still producing.*
Scaffolds —
 thick lower arms,
 split
 clean through to daylight;
 brittle as shard, their
 bark, burned, scarred
 from years of swing rope,
 whisper

 *We*
 *drew laughter from children.*

 \* \* \* \*

Some say this favoured Nashwaak ground
was Appleseed's only Canadian
stop.

*Johnny slept here —*
*only one night on his way to Ohio,*
*but*
*planted these trees himself.*
Some say it's foolish
    *— The dates are all wrong —*
others hold the visit
as fact.
Whichever is true,
facts can be sown, can be
scattered, as seed,
farther afield than demanded
by need,
thinking by tripling
up on the feed,

something's
bound to take root.

# 1878 – 1896
# Bucksaw and Plough

This is where he settled
that spring of '78 —
high ground
off the Nashwaak River, though
Gagetown was
the place to be. When
cleared of stump and stone,
this field of second choice would grow
to forty acres plus,
and a hundred more
of timberland
was his if he would work the soil.
First thing
Michael Maguire did

was plant his apple seeds.

    \* \* \* \*

He'd come in the Second Wave
— after the Scots —
out of Ireland: Enniskillen,
County of Fermanagh.
The island was one country then,
though
none would say without troubles:
outliers' lips,
outlanders' hands from pocket to throat,
seized,
squeezed,
extracted their due —
nutrient sucked from the mouths of babes
for the puffing of pastries

in London — her cuffs
and collars of lace.
He'd sworn in a public place;
had demanded the landowner
pay him a wage.
Not his first time found
in a fix.
> *Come now, Paddy-boy,*
> *you'd better take stock;*
> *consider how gracious I be.*
> *Careful*
> *you don't play the man.*
> *Better you not stand your ground,*
> *than stand to lose*
> *the ground you have.*

He listened. Took stock. Weighed
life in the balance.
Light, found, is a marvellous thing,
save when it defines *your* side
of the scale.
Michael — never married —
snuck away to the pier,

set sail for a country
called *Canada.*

\* \* \* \*

He petitioned
for a grant on the high ground
east of this river
the Maliseet call *slow current.*
Half the first cut was turned into board;
second half, into a jenny.

Built an oversized shed he
split
with a wall —
bigger half went to the mule.
Ed Irwin, from down
on the riverbank, said
> *That's just how marriage works —*
> *like it does with me and Maggie.*
> *'Half' is always three to one*
> *— never one, two, three; no logic —*
> *but no man's yet*
> *found a happy way around it.*

Ed wandered in every few weeks;
boasted that
he
was the head of the house —
well fit to craft Michael
in all arts domestic;
could teach him
the skills men so desperately need
but oh, so evidently
lack —
how to pick that perfect
four-leafed clover
hidden in a field of shamrock.
Lessons would be free
should Michael guarantee
Ed would be home
by 5:43, that minute
Maggie made him

> *Sit down*
> *to supper!*

\* \* \* \*

Michael
and Biddy worked the ground,
not half as hard as they could have.
He liked to fish,
she liked the shade —
no sense
sweating away the *whole*
afternoon.
Long as Biddy's carrots got planted;
long as Michael's trees
got pruned before May,
this was Life,
and Life was good —

and soon to be better
with apples.

\* \* \* \*

The days of promise
dropped upon them —
an orchard in the high field,
heavy, and branched
to family lines:
first pick to Michael and Biddy,
then to the Johnstons,
the Gallaghers and Byrnes;
to the Irwins on the flats
where frosts would lie —
some years
as late as early
June

they'd see their blossoms
burn:

no blossoms,
no apples;

no apples,
no deer;

no deer,
no suet;

no suet,
no tallow;

no tallow,
no soap;

no soap,
no courting —

no one the apple
of anyone's eye.

  * * * *

He gave no thought
to the cough,
to the blood.
 *Just dust,*
he said.
The night sweats bothered him most —
dreams on a loop of howls and cackles,
falls from a cliff,
a windmill of limbs through an ether of bubbles.

The Doc couldn't tell him
why his weight was
down;
his workdays, too —
three hours, tops.
> *'Nough for now, Mule.*
> *We'll finish tomorrow.*
> *There will always be another day.*
Three weeks behind in the planting.
Carrot seed
still
on the kitchen table.
Michael wrote the letter
in duplicate:
one for James in Enniskillen,
one for the judge in Fredericton.
The consumption didn't stop
til it killed him,
but the letters came to life
when he died —
their voice, official:

nephew James
to have the farm.

# 1897 – 1902
## The brave, to the New Land …

James and Sarah
Maguire,
five children and
Mona, James' widowed sister
in tow.
All she had
tied up
in nieces and nephews, her
fool husband, Dougal,
gone;
not from the sickness,
not lost at sea —
no battlefield honours for one
turned thug; this
knave, transparent,
ever dripping in wax
to hide the cracks; he
fooled all the people, and that,
all the time,
though quite another story with his
one-eyed horse —

Gilley Boy
saw clear through him.

    \* \* \* \*

They didn't sail from Belfast —
fires having set
the docks long into repairs.
Another route of passage?
The *State of Nebraska*
— to leave Londonderry —
could land them on Ellis Island.

Not where they wanted to go —
reports of cholera,
and second class, only a dream.
So it was "out of Dublin Town"
for those with nothing left —
though a fair port she was then,
fairer than most,
for should ever a freshening, contrary wind
come blowing in hard 'cross the bay,
she'd drive a quick ship on to Liverpool,

and one, from there,
could seize the world.

\* \* \* \*

Theirs was not a coffin ship —
two hundred souls stuffed
into holds,
pining on bunks
in the bowels of steerage,
drippings
shared
with the bed below.
Little light, less air —
who could live there?
No response from three in ten —
from the one hundred thousand who perished.
Over in a splash,
shark-trains in tow.
Few ships to be found
like the prized *Jeanie Johnston* —
a captain who cared,

a surgeon on call, east to west
a dozen times. With the twenty-five hundred
she carried,
not a passenger lost at sea.
James was in hopes of the same —
this ship, iron,
driven by steam;
he and his family
— not fifty
days —

only twelve
til Halifax rose from the sea.

\* \* \* \*

Forty-three acres.
Land, sufficient.
Water, ever a chore.
Abundant, but had to be
bucketed
clear
from the pool fed full by the spring
just over the hill
and through the grove,
across the flats and back again,
six circuits every day.
Saturdays,
nine.
    *We must be clean for church,*
she'd say.
Skin
scrubbed red.

*We want ears that squeak*
*on heads of*
*silent boys.*

*Yes, Mother.*

\* \* \* \*

Every tree felled —
more worth than Wicklow gold:
pasture gained for horse and mules,
hewn lumber for houses and sheds,
fuel, split green, long
ranked for warming fires.
Board wood, rough
for table and bench.
Bird's-eye, the cherished:
planed, sanded,
caressed to silk and lined with felt —
a little box to hide her
secret things.
The same, true of stone.
Each one taken
deepened the foundation and
raised the height of the wall.
The riddle of rock
when pulled from its grave —
how the hole in the ground

fills the same
in the heart.

\* \* \* \*

Logs carted out
to the mill on the stream near Killarney.
Trunks
trundled in,
lumber retrieved,
two hours each way with a horse;
three if pulled by the mules.
Stubborn things.
Though he'd never hit one
with a shovel,

he threatened to dig many
a hole.

    \* \* \* \*

    *You're growing your herd?*
    *Then you're needin' a house,*
    *and sooner than later,*
said the man at the mill, sawyer Tom.
    *This livin' in sheds*
    *—fine in a pinch, but*
    *twenty years here have taught me*
    *you can't keep it up into snow.*
He'd take a tenth of the total
in cash,
up front,
    *But only if your children*
    *have warm winter coats.*
The remainder would wait
for the harvests' take,
or he'd settle the difference in stock.

*Sheaves of barley, or straw,
or lambs, come spring.
I always need lambs.
Are the coyotes circlin' your fields?
I've caught them scoutin' my pens.*
Tom was down in stock,
his wife, wanting
in wool.
*Or apples,*
he said,
*you can
promise me apples
— whatever you have I will take —
but we need to get you out
of the cold.*

Sawyer Tom — a straighter man
than he whose name stood flipped.

* * * *

A cow went down
October the eighth,
nine thirty-five Tuesday morning.
Bellowed, bawled,
front legs locked up,
lay gurgling in foam.
Not a soul could be found
who could say why she dropped.
Single heifer, but double
the loss —
none dared eat the meat.
That fall they moved into

a twenty-by-twenty house,
the shed handed back
to the now
— at last —

contented
cows.

      \* \* \* \*

Wasn't much to it
— squared wooden frame,
off-centred patches of glass.
Roof topped in clear cedar shakes.
Walls with only half their fill —
horsehair tossed in buckwheat hulls.
You could feel what wasn't there,
December days of thirty below,
the warmest ones of January.
Not a spare minute to covet the Jones',
life's bar
set at *survival*.
No Franklin stove;
only a fireplace gorging spruce
and gnarls of yellow birch —
all it could eat
to heat the sky.
Stones
from the hearth to the beds.
Children
hugging the chimney,

warm long after
the embers had died.

# 1897 – 1902
…the tortured, to follow

James had family back home.
Two of three sisters
married twin brothers
— Reillys — from the farm
that straddled River Erne.
Each bore a daughter:
Shannon, to Mary and Peter,
Hannah, to Neasa and Paul;
made the girls cousins
though all would say 'sisters'
who saw them
together:
two of a mind,
two of a soul,
two, the one,
two, the whole.
Fingers slit
to blended blood,

> *We shall be sisters*
> *forever.*

\* \* \* \*

Dougal lost the cottage in Drumcoo,
in the grove half a mile behind
Enniskillen,
six months behind
on the rent
money
gone to drink.
He and Mona
— could have no children —
came to live at Hannah's house.

Hannah loved her Aunt Mona
and was glad to see Dougal
bring the horses.
She fought to be kind
and could be
at times,
for, sober, he was a horseman —
no man in the counties
his equal.
But civility towards him, a strain
for Hannah,
eased only by distance
or solitude —
her custom to slip away
to the heath.

Tragic that habits
are picked up by others.

    * * * *

Clouds hung in mizzled misery
above the whisted moor;
crept
as smoke rolls, crests
enfolding
Hannah in scents
of heather:
earthy, woody, tones of musk,
her basket on her arm.
    *What's that?*
Twigs snap.
    *Who's there?*
Silence.

Hushed from behind,
a hand to her mouth,
head driven, forced
in the heath,
pinioned
in a muffle of screams.
She ripped a posy from the earth,
pressed it to her nose,
drew deep
— essence of delicate her means of escape;
sailed her into that haven
of *anywhere-but-here*.
Ravished in the fens,
but Hannah wasn't there —
wasn't where she was that day

Dougal
stalked the moor.

\* \* \* \*

By near-blood betrayed,
violated — trust
and person.
Found
by fingers emboldened.
Another emptied bottle thrown
from hands that
had
— and ever would —
in dry times
war to shield her.

She didn't tell
Neasa. She couldn't
tell Paul — her
parents must never know.
She would stay behind the wall,
reach through the bars,
reset life to the shadows,
hold self as unclean —
bear the blame, would
keep herself from becoming,

lest her family be smeared
with shame.

  * * * *

Bugs scent distress
in weakened trees —
sets them thinking
 *Easy prey.*
Deluded, they,
not knowing plants' defences.
Their first bite triggers alarms —
trees sound silent warnings:
from canopy
a chemistry, and
from their feeder roots entwined
with others in the grove,
a cry to raise their guard:
 *Initiate defences.*
Leaf skins thicken.
Hannah, calloused
yet standing —

a sweet bay tree yet
standing,
though no longer green,

and no more beside
still waters.

    * * * *

Ripples, now —
refracting bent, bruised
beams of light,
Hannah, a ghost in the making;
nebulous outline,
aqueous tomb —
a spectre
in suspension, not wanting
to sink, fearing
to surface.
This was not the girl
that was — reflection, clear
in pools serene —
now splintered into composites:
iron — brittle, cold —
no longer fused with Adam's clay.
Many offered a shoulder, but
— Shannon excepted —

Hannah bore the burden
alone.

    * * * *

Lavender.
Dianthus.
Wintergreen mint,
favourite perennial perfumes.
But the Everlasting was Hannah's
flower —
a bloom with cousins in Family Asteraceae:
one, Pearly;
two, Mountain;
three, an Everlasting called Life.
Hannah's flower — Life Everlasting.

She breathed its essence
and wished for death.

   \* \* \* \*

Horses,
Dougal had three.
Two young Cobs — a matched pair,
all he knew of balance.
The third, an Irish Draught —
burly, deep-chested,
full sixteen hands high.
Eye — single, yet
fire and blood;
nostrils — a furnace of steam.
But spooked in a storm of thunder and flash,
Gilley Boy reared, tore away;
Fool Dougal, hell-bent
on reigning him in.
Tangled, tight
in twisted cord,

pinned under a wild and
driving flank, but
onlookers swore they had witnessed
a deliberate synchronization
of pounding stomps and snorts.
If not Divine retribution,
then, equine

justice,
meted from a horse.

# 1903 – 1905
# Flowers and Whispers

One-and-twenty years
inseparable,
til that April day on a Dublin dock.
There was only a month
between them;
soon to be a month
and an ocean.
Hannah's
escape:
> *It's now.*
> *I must go.*
> *They have told me.*
Said she saw
signs — pieces
of rainbow, burning
either side of the western
sun — her hopes hung
high;
parhelion sky.
No one told her of sundogs.
Two
faces in tears, but

Shannon said she understood
why.

\* \* \* \*

Hannah, away,
took ship to Saint John —
a trip to remember.
Not everyone would.
Arrived,
but died within the year —

one of the lucky ones under a curse. Was
said she flitted her sea-
blue eyes
at the deck-hand lowering the lifeboat.
Cast him a wink,
puddled him to pudding;
played him with a promise
she knew she'd never pay.
Completely
out of character.
Desperation does strange things.
Sinking in a Fundy gale
can leach the good from anyone.
While she did not die with the others
— didn't drown when the ship slipped
under the waves — that
seat in the dinghy would sink her.
Ten strokes pulled them to safety,
to a view of the deck lined with leftover children
screaming, clutching the rails.
The tempest muted the cries, but
it could not hide
the faces
even when downed in the Deep.
Whose seat had she stolen?
Which child, displaced?
Images
burned.
    *If thy right eye offend thee ...*
Plucked from the waves,

to the end of her days
held under.

    \* \* \* \*

> *Women and children only!*
> *Sorry, Miss. No luggage.*

Hannah made it to shore with what she could hide,
beaded handbag strapped to her thigh.
Thirty shillings for a two-dollar ticket
— the steamer, *Victoria* —
up the St. John to the Fredericton wharf,
carriage
from there to the high ground —
to James' and Sarah's,
to cousins Maguire, five
years since last seen.
Time quenches no flame. The brood
encircles.

> *Hannah! You made it!*
> *You're sharing Sylvie's room.*
> *Yes,* Sylvia squealled, *you're with me.*
> *And Mother has made us a quilt!*
> She grabbed Hannah's hand.
> *Come see.*

Welcoming.
Warm.
A gift: one of Sylvia's dresses.
This was her family away.
Yet ...
too little of something, too
much
of another, she could not
frame all the pieces;
she couldn't hold on.
Hannah Reilly, dead
at twenty-two,

was never able
to sleep.

    \* \* \* \*

Shannon had received
the letters:
Hannah's writings —
>  her life in New Brunswick away
>  from the moor.
>  *I see much more of the sun,*
>  *but, Shannon, I can't*
>  *outrun*
>  *the clouds.*

Two months later,
the letter from Sarah and James —
>  *Hannah is dead.*
>  *We last saw her leaving church.*
>  *When the preacher proclaimed*
>  *"If any man thirst ..."*
>  *she whispered*
>  *she wished*
>  *a drink from the spring.*
>  *The Irwins found her next to the pool,*
>
>  *her Bible*
>  *opened to Psalm 23.*

    \* \* \* \*

A scar on Shannon's finger —
all she had left to hold
of that April day on the dock,
their last day together, now
two years gone.

She could not speak of her yet
in eyes unveiled of tears —
two young girls on the moor,
Shannon, weaving ribbons in dark ginger locks:
one, blue,
for sky — immeasurable
soul;
one, yellow,
for sun ever-rising.
No one could trace Hannah's smile.
Though freckles run scattered
through patchworks of pink
— adornments erratically sown —
hers had been patterned with purpose:
crescents of cinnamon
edging to opal, set

soft
in cheeks of tan.

    \* \* \* \*

May saw another Dublin ship
dock at Partridge Island,
inner harbour off Saint John.
Shannon aboard,
with Stewie —
to make their way up river.
Two days
turned into twenty,
the fault entirely her own.
Disembarking, she chanced to sneeze;
found herself posted in quarantine.

She
came through fine — bit harder
on the dog.
Good thing for Stewie
the trunk was full of holes —

whimpers
finding him a friend.

  * * * *

Arrived three weeks late
at Maguire's farm,
Aunt Sarah out sweeping the steps.
Shannon kissed her and ran
to the plot —
four fieldstones enclosed
in a white picket fence.
No rest for her
til she knelt at Hannah's grave —
a year's worth of whispers
to share with her friend.
 *I've brought you something from home.*
She lifted the roots from her basket —
Hannah's flowers from Fermanagh;
clumps of Everlasting —
second cousin to edelweiss.
Tears in courses,
thumbs caressing
as one would stroke a fledgling
fallen from its nest.
She parted the clumps
secured in muslin,
damp with scent

of summers spent
running through the heath —
Shannon, collecting her flowers;
Hannah, transforming

from butterfly
to worm.

    \* \* \* \*

A circle round Hannah's stone —
Shannon planted virgin whites
with spills of bloody pink;
roots of *he*
and roots of *she*,
for with the Everlastings
— Pearly, Mountain, Life —
both *hes* and *shes* are needed
for flowers
full
to bloom.
Life everlasting,
dioecious.
This field never held the sisters together.
Hannah, here
little more than a year,

her death, too soon
from sleep too late.

# 1906 – 1939
Under the sun

News by word-of-mouth.
Bits from the school,
bits from the pulpit, the
bulk
dispersed by the miller,
his wheel ever-grinding,
endless
streams of corn.
Some news, familial:
> *An upcoming marriage*
> *for Kathleen and Connor.*
> His first,
> her second,
> her first having died of diphtheria.
> When Connor carried her
> over the threshold,
> he suppressed a smile
> and sang,
> *I take you home AGAIN Kathleen.*
Some news, spiritual:
> *The second Sunday of September, we will hold*
> *a picnic.*
> But to ward off certain charges
> of Sabbath desecration …
> *Young Emma Byrne will be baptized.*
> *Her senior sister, Molly*
> *will recite, in toto,*
> *Second Timotheus, Chapter Three:*
> *From a child thou hast known*
> *Holy Scriptures,*
> *able to make thee wise unto salvation*
> *through faith which is in*
> *Jesus Christ.*

Did well for a shy girl of nine.
Stumbled only
a single time —

her new shoes catching
the foot of the pulpit.

\* \* \* \*

Lynch; O'Neill —
dark Fenians marching to silent strains
of *Éirinn go Brách* — Ireland Forever.
Though their cause took a hit in the raids,
all was not lost —
Edward Lynch weaseling his way
down to Eastport,
joined the Maine Brotherhood,
battle cry:
    *Torch Campobello!*
A pity their weapons were seized.
Took seven hundred men
to capture the Custom House flag.
Ed slithered home.
Kept his mouth shut, told all
who'd missed him
his great-grandma's sister down Bar Harbor way
had sure been happy to see him.
He died that July;
body, under meadow,
spirit
— underground factions live still —
restless until it descended upon
his grandson Paul, and compatriots —
lived out the ruse to blend in.

Victoria Day,
the most difficult day of the year.
Potatoes, planted;
fences, mended —
patriots, all;
to rest,
wave flags;
a glass

> *To Her Majesty the Queen;*
> *To the Empire,*

a murmured toast
through gritted teeth —
this cadre to the Republic
sworn
to take up arms in the overthrow, yet
certain to smile
whenever Maguire came knocking,
bearing gifts —
a share of his harvest;
a bushel of his best from an outstretched hand.

> *Just something good*
> *neighbours should do.*

\* \* \* \*

Wee Willy Newly —
more than a handful, born
a hefty twelve-ten,
two pounds a week after that.
Sober-minded while in school —
after class, never
gave a thought to the day.
Played hooky once.

Even that dropped out of the blue —
never planned to go fishing.
A laid-back sort;
fell asleep when the trout did the same.
Slid an inch down the bank with every snore.
The day they found his body,
his mom hacked the pole to pieces;
burnt them on the river bank.
The next windy day

she flung the ashes
from the top of the hill.

\* \* \* \*

The day they lowered Willy into the ground,
came the report of rifles
from Europe.
Canadian boys
in the tens, then hundreds,
of thousands
soon lined the trenches —
same years the spuds turned to mush.
Men could fight the blight
on either side of the ocean.
Young, restless,
naïve,
many wouldn't pick
the potato,

or come home
when the rifle shots ended.

\* \* \* \*

Cities were hit the hardest.
Farms — at first — took less of a punch,
though time, moving on, drove
men into doing the same.
From fields
to factories,
to riding the rails,
half the country removed
from home;
half the homes in the settlement,
reft.
And with the pall overspreading the land,

even plough-boys
would feel the Depression.

* * * *

The summer of '37
brought forth her cups and quarts —
well on her way
to bushels of promise, when,
come the first week of July,
half-inch through, pale blue
ice stones of thunderhail
would buckshot all that was green.
Growing season now
on the far side of late.
Would she yield a second crop?
Give a six-week Indian summer?
No choice but to plant again.
Moulding seed.
What a teaser she was!

*Possibly*
slid into *maybe;*
*maybe* into
*looks like she might.*
But just as *she is*
was nearing *she will,*
one night of killer frost,
and twenty-eight days of rheumatic fever.
Many,
weakened,
saw their hearts damaged;

others
lost theirs entirely.

# 1940 – 1952
# The weight of a straw

Few remember why
Daniel Maguire
was late coming home from the camps —
four months deep
in Miramichi
felling black spruce, white
pine, logs
yarded,
stacked
three men high on the skidways.
But breakup came early that year.
He told Cooky to leave the corned beef,
three pounds of coffee and
ten of potatoes. He could
feed himself for a week.
And he wouldn't be missed on the drive —
not a runner; no skill in his feet.
He'd be fine on his own, though his
soul yearned for Millie —
their peanut butter picnics,
and porch swing ginger beer
sunsets.
But he'd not break camp
til his carving was done.

> *And a few days alone*
> *always does a man good.*

\* \* \* \*

No mail drops.
No way for news to reach him.
He finished the carving
and all of the grub —

half a pound short on the coffee.
Came home
to his Millie,
to a premature son,
to his Millie and a breech-birthed boy,
both four days in the ground,
She had dictated a note.
The midwife
left it pinned to his pillow.

> *My darling Daniel,*
>     *How I miss you. I'm having some pain today. Jenny's been here helping with the chores; giving me backrubs.*
>     *I feel the baby all the time now — kicks under my ribs. Is it possible our child's already wearing boots?*
>     *Sadie came last night. She can stay for the week, provided Alice Byrne doesn't come to term.*
>     *I like the name Rachel; or if a boy, Benoni, after her son. Stay near me, my Daniel. I have you in my heart. You owe me a swing come blossom-time. We'll have gingers again on the porch. Forever your love,*
>
>     *Millie*

\* \* \* \*

Storm winds on dark water. Night
pressed upon soul
riven through;
blade, driven,
deep, thrusted twist of a hollowing fire —
clean to the haft,
to the heart.

Staggered, but would not fall.
>*Not yet,*
he muttered.
>*You'll not go yet,*
>*Dan Maguire.*

>*One last thing to be done.*

\* \* \* \*

Chiselled in rock:
>*Here lies my wife*
>MILLIE MAGUIRE
>*1918–1940*
>*and BENONI*
>*son of my sorrow*
>*They died while I was gone*

His neighbours said not to —
the last line would grow
to haunt him.
They would find him another stone.
His face, set as flint:
>*I need a place to go;*
>*to where I can talk;*
>*to where I can say I'm sorry;*
>*can forever say I am sorry.*

None could deny him that right.
And none there were who wanted to,
but no one could recall
him saying,

>*A stone to speak*
>*when I'm gone.*

\* \* \* \*

His legs would not hold him —
crumpled, convulsing, he
wielded a fist in a surge of damnations,
beat on the granite
til three cracked bones
forced his hands into feathered strokes,
fingers drawn down a body
of stone —
caresses that could not hold her.
On her grave, a spray of dogwood
— she loved red, and April holds no roses —
and from the white pine
behind
the lumber camp's horse shed —

the sleigh he had carved
for the child.

\* \* \* \*

He refused
invitations to supper;
let nobody in — found
dishes dropped off at his door.
First days, in stacks,
dwindled as the weeks wore on,
though a fresh loaf of bread
could appear anytime.
Neighbours kicked in:
cut his wood, weeded when he
snuck
into town for supplies.

Hard for Dan to take
acts of kindness;
anything
gifted.
They missed him at church.
All agreed:

> *That poor man.*
> *Just needs time.*

\* \* \* \*

He never made it back
to the spirit he was;
anyone could see it —
drained eyes in rote,
a snuffed wick, life's
flame — not to embers
reduced, but —
fizzled,
cold
into powder of ash.
Doc ran some tests: said
> *Everything's fine, but*
> *here, Dan, take this elixir —*
> *one teaspoon with meals.*
> *Two with dessert.*

And the Reverend found little
to point to.
Dan, pressed between,
swallowed them both, but
religion could draw nothing
out;

medicine
could put nothing in.
Sinking,
adrift —
everything the only thing
wrong.
But Sweeney, the druggist, said he
understood;
had deciphered the cause from Dan's
own hand; from shopping lists
shoved cross the counter —
screams heard
from words not there.
    *Millie's seven years gone,*
said Sweeney,
then read back the list to Dan —
    *Barbituates.*
    *Benzedrine sulphate.*

    *But never a bottle*
    *of ginger beer.*

\* \* \* \*

The Maguire farm had fallen
by the fall of '52.
Last man gone, the field
deserted, restored to living
alone;
only the north wind pushing the swing,
sounding
wrinkled tin on the shed.

Brambles and
roses and
vines of frost grape,
tendril-and-thorn opportunists,
land
envelopers,
strangling house and
barn, both abandoned
after niece
Fiona

found Daniel hanged
from a rafter.

1952 – 2017
The loss of full circle

Most call this a wasteland.
Seventy years fallow,
its only production —
intangibles:
night-sound concertos:
> *An Evening of Owl Whistle* — sharp, though
> in dull, minor keys.
> *Mockingbirds' Thievery* — robin
> and jay.
> *Coyote Operas* — in multiple tracks.

And such pageantry
modelled
on celestial runways:
> *Motions*
> *of Moon-Sail* —
> She lifts
> her veil, slips
> into a robe of gossamer silk,
> spangles her train in stardust.
> Quickens her breath
> into breezes —
> treetop caresses,
> undulating
> waves, silvered
> shivers;
> mercurial
> webworks of lace.

What would have been Eden's
displays?

  \* \* \* \*

But to others, this meadow's green
rises,
blends into blue where, with wind
under wing, the eagle,
in updraft,
unruffled,
soars.
A squadron of crows pours
out of the sun,
rat-a-tat-tats the intruder
with caws,
> *This is*
> *our*
> *section of sky.*
Pesters him into a flap
of descent —
Beelzebub's demons,

ever a-thirst,
brook satisfaction in none.

  * * * *

Daniel's farm ran next to his brother's —
Thomas, father of Fiona
and Jack.
*Jack* — not his real name;
a handle he took for a joke.
To his family he was always
Collin;
had to quit from the strain on his throat.
Rode two miles a day
twice a day

those winter months Daniel
was working the camps.
Watered Millie's cattle.
Did what chores needed done.
And for the twelve years Daniel
half-lived alone,
Jack's horse spent all
its walking hours

on the trail
between the farms

  * * *

Millie, gone.
Benoni, gone.
Daniel, buried in shame.
House but a shell of echoes,
Jack said
Ontario
looked good to him.
A passenger train to Toronto.
Jumped off early, some forty
miles shy.
Heard the country was
needing more cars,
was wanting more cars — was
so drunk on cars, the
plants were paying
one-eighty an hour to build them.
Jack worked the line
at GM in Oshawa,

til Ford
came to Oakville in '53.

\* \* \* \*

Phone calls and letters —
mainly, letters.
Who could afford long distance?
No one on this end.
Took twelve long years
for Jack to get back to this high ground.
Arrived
unannounced
in the summer of '64.
    *Made it in eighteen hours,*
he said,
patting the hood of his Mustang.
    *Only twenty-four hundred dollars.*
    *That's near a year's wages*
    *down here.*
    *And I play the guitar now, too.*
No one asked for a song,
but he
brought it along to the campfire.
Brutalized a cover of *I Wanna Hold Your Hand*,
though he did a good job
on the other one —
burned it to a peel
when he stumbled into the flames.
Snapped the Martin in half on a birch stump —
neck,
broke from the body, still
hung with strings.
Pushed him over the line —
Hammer Toss time at the Highland
Games.

Spun three revolutions then
planted his heels,
launched it into the trees.
Margy came with butter and gauze.
Jack winced with every loop.
*I'll be leaving in the morning,*
he said.
Stared at the circle of faces.
*How do you people
live like this?*
Mounties called the next afternoon.

*Could someone come to Grand Falls?
Identify a body?*

\* \* \* \*

The house no longer stands.
Lumber's all but disappeared —
in with a horse,
out with a truck;
pieces pillaged,
peeled away.
Those boards were sacred
once: enclosed
survival's inner sanctum,
sheltered souls
— and if no one woke the wind —
raised thirty-below to the melting point,
nursed them through
to a rising sun.
Gone now,
ripped from the grip
of rusted spikes,

pilfered away,
scabbed to the walls
of the man-caves of profligates;
who live for their senses

yet cannot hear the howls
in the wood.

 \* \* \* \*

John says the old house
blew away.
I tell him he is crazy
but I think he could be right —
any piece not stolen, torn
from the trusses,
lifted
long ago by the wind.
You can see where it stood.
This foundation of stones?
to cradle the wood laid upon it.
Never lay sill upon soil.
Even hemlock will rot
touching mud.
Set your sills upon stone.
Build upon rock
and you'll pay little mind to the storms.
But is there nothing
here? No trinket,
no bauble entombed for one lost soul
who might, perchance
— just passing by —
stop to kick at stones?

No redeeming relic
for a seeker
born too late?
That swing on dancing rope —
two girdling rings
worn smooth

from generations of underducks.

\* \* \* \*

Mrs. Estey remembers.
Says her mother spoke of gravestones,
seven near the southern line —
that hardpan swath
where the oats wouldn't take;
no feed for the horses,
though one can see tracts of coltsfoot.
Seven stones.
No one knows where they are
today —
sepulchres sunk in sanded clay,

the soil one needs
growing apples.

\* \* \* \*

I don't believe this field wants to die,
though she does lie
poisoned — concentrations
of salt; sweat-
drops from hard labour
— there's always a harvest of rocks —
and festered pools of secret tears,

the run-off
of hobbled dreams:
never
to daub brushes on canvas;
never
to pen worlds on a page.
There was wood to haul
and beef to corn
and fruit to pick and
put up in bottles; potatoes
and turnips
to put down in cellars of earth —
kept dry, not to mould;
kept moist, not to wither;
kept cool, not to freeze — in hopes of forestalling
invasions of alien worms —
those softening, life-sucking
sprouts.
Ah, but what sweet, soothing pangs
of conscience, when
— house entombed in February snow,
trees mummied in ice —
there, cozied next to the fire,
one indulged such
florid ambrosia:

a dish of pumpkin
preserves.

    \* \* \* \*

I do not
believe
this field wants to die. June

spreads herself in strawberries,
July, droops of fruit,
in raspberries, hung.
August unfolds her blankets of blues, her
blackberries shared with September.
She doesn't want to die,
and she battles to prove it:
Reds hold the ground to the North;
Blacks entrenched to the West;
Blues, encamped on the Eastern Front,
seized another acre
in last year's advance.

The Colours of War.
Always in season.

\* \* \* \*

Seedling spruce.
All of an age, identically girthed,
as sentries posted,
stand.
Unarmed as yet.
But needles
stiffen —
ten years on they'll be lancers.
To come to one's
purpose may take some time —
unlike these ash volunteers
who out
will sprout
from anywhere.
They love to be cursed —
the way they sneak up

between these stones;
will split them if they have to;

will split them if they
want to.

    \* \* \* \*

I've just been told:
this old foundation has moved
from holding up
a frontier house
to holding up
development.
They want to bring the dozers in.
> *Time to peel the berries back — to take*
> *the sand for drainage;*
> *for multiple lines of various kinds*
> *to be hung on a grove of poles:*
> *lines, electric, lines*
> *buried for gas,*
> *lines so the world*
> *can reach us.*
> *Houses, sardined,*
> *perched on this ridge —*
>
> *each*
> *with its million-dollar view.*

    \* \* \* \*

Just had a chat with Bobby and Lil.
I mentioned the price.
> *A million?*

says Lil,

all the while
leaping at butterflies.
>    *Dollars?*
Bob scratches;
>    *Is that what you said?*
>    *A million to purchase this field?*
They pause from their play
to confer.
Lil's the one
voted
spokesperson for two:
>    *As far as buying*
>    *this field for its view,*
>    *we can see such a sum being offered*
>    *by any so poor*
>    *as to not yet have seen it.*

Dogs make
most sense
most times.

\* \* \* \*

These brambles, I can pull
— drooping, thorny sceptre heads —
with just a single yank.
But saplings —
up through cracks in stone,
anchored in a firmer stance —
take a double-handed haul.
As this one growing
through the wall —
to cut it back,
you'd only gain a week or two.

With its fifty feet of fibrous root
now forcing buds
to flush to shoots
of mottled stems
in brindled brown —
returning with
a second crown of even thicker green.
I wedge a stick beneath:
jimmy, wiggle, scratch
and claw,
I clean unearth its feet —

mine,
now buried in rock.

* * * *

Stones
versus shins.
Stones win; set me back
on my haunches.
Eyes catch a glint
from the hollow in the wall.
Flakes of iron
over grey;
flecked, mirrored
specks in clay,
a tin, exposed:
Sweet Caporal Tobacco.
Bottom rusted, top
encrusted — this
is no deterrent to

a seeker
born to pry.

\* \* \* \*

Newspaper
snippets unearthed.
Tin in hand,
in the other, my foot,
bloodied,
bruised from the fall.
Pyrrhic victory, this —
reading news of a century past
to a wounded massaging
of toes.
History stuffed
in snuffs of tobacco.
Headlines filtered
on papers now stained smokers' yellow.
Years past
in a puff.

Years
passed in a puff.

\* \* \* \*

Clippings:
    January 1904,
    top of page three.
    Marconi picking
    a frequency;
    Chekov — an orchard of cherries,
    red orbs in a future Red Square.
Clippings:
    pages one and two, missing;
    four through twenty, nowhere to be found.

Their loss would make little difference,
for all of the pages
in all of the world
would have to be rewritten —

two brothers from Dayton
had left the Earth.

\* \* \* \*

Scrawlings shoved into tin.
Sheets torn,
stripped from spools of butcher's wrap;
writings on the side not coated
in wax —
unprotected,
sporadically smeared in blood,
inscribed in the dark
lead of pencil,
blurred with the smudges of tears —
mind of a poet from
soul of a child.
Discomfited now,
I shift;
pull myself to a stand.
Uncomfortable still
— these papers in hand —

> *Aren't the hearts of children*
> *supposed to be free?*

\* \* \* \*

Hannah's letter to Shannon —
heart of gold
in a box of tin:
> *I hate that sea of pink*
> *out there.*
> *Held under; pressed to earth.*
> *Would to God*
> *that man had slit my throat.*
> *Runs of blood down my neck*
> *would have raised*
> *their stares. My snips*
> *were there in the basket!*
> *I've lain in the darkness of Luz —*
> *been forced*
> *to pillow with Jacob,*
> *though mine, of harder stone.*
> *There was no ladder for me*
> *to climb,*
> *no faeries descended to help.*
> *Though two heard my screams,*
> *not one heard my prayer.*
> *I cannot lay me down to sleep,*
> *there being none to keep*
> *my soul. My mattress stinks*
> *of heather.*
> *No matter; the floor*
> *serves me well —*
>
> *a quicker crawl*
> *into a hole.*

\* \* \* \*

This stone foundation is all that's left — this
half of a hole in the ground.
Footprints of five generations wiped
clean, memories
scrubbed, graves,
lost.
Ploughed over?
Ploughed under? Far worse —
ploughed through;
not as a blade into sod
— that promise of life infused when nurturing seed —
this breach, a plough
into snow —
shoves aside, pushes
to peripheries.
*Move over! It's dawned a new day.*
*Plastic for metal. Pressed*
*sawdust for wood.*
*From dining room tables to television*
*trays —*
*dinners in the den;*
*conversation —*
*full meal to piecemeal,*
*background noise to Channel 4;*
*Channel 2 if the cloud cover's right.*
Twice-a-year coats of whitewash,
twice-a-week treatments of lime;
a sunflower jungle of five-hundred heads —
euphemisms
ornament the outhouse;
gravestones, let go to sand.
The unearthing of Self:

not,
> *We are better than
> this,*

but,

> *We
> are better than they.*

\* \* \* \*

Trees do not heal
themselves.
They leave an injury as is —
grow around the hurt
in search of an alternate path;
reconnect life-forces
just over there
beyond the perimeter of pain.
Scars remain
forever —
not so, the absence of fruit.
Apples will grow again.
Shade from heat.
Courage from cuts.

Such a comfort,
trees.

\* \* \* \*

Stand with me here. Come closer..
See how the ridge runs
down to the vale — where that dark balsam stand
trails thick to the knoll?

Down by the…
Wait! In the orchard!
There's One who's come to call.
Those four pioneers
— cankered with rot;
bark skinned, limbs,
thin, draped in swags
of moss —

they know
who He is.

* * * *

The creep of Death in the high ground;
He slithers through the stand,
rears up and
straightens His tie.
Says,
    *This is no trespass.*
    *I go where I want.*
Sweeps that knuckle-knotted finger
in claim across the grove.
He sees us watching.

Slings a smirk
from under His hood.

* * * *

    *Then do it, Death; take them —*
    *all four if You like.*
    *They've served their time well —*
    *homesteaders who've earned*

*their sleep.*
*They've spent their seed,*
*and those they nourished*
*said* thank you *years ago.*
*You bluster,*
*You boast, but You threaten*
*no sting;*
*not to these stalwarts — these*
*anchors of time and place.*
*You're late. For they have come*
*to where they can die.*

*And I've come to where*
*I can let them go.*

\* \* \* \*

*This field's in good hands.*
*That sapling there?*
*And there?*
*Three more,*
*and beyond?*
*I know You can see them —*
*green, growing,*

*young ones coming up everywhere.*

# Acknowledgements

Though writing is surely a solitary work, on this journey from thought to book-in-hand, many fellow travelers have come alongside.

I want to thank...

my Fictional Friends writers group, for their many helpful suggestions. "Don't lose your voice, but what if you said it this way...?"

Gwen, for first-eyes on the poem. "There's something here, Neil."

Lorna and John, for standing with me in the field, pointing out how things used to be. "The graveyard was over there. No. Over there."

Janet, for finding the old pictures. And for her notes to *And the River Rolled On...Two Hundred Years on the Nashwaak*, a New Brunswick bicentennial publication. "You can keep these as long as you like."

Nancy and Deb, for letting us walk their field. For sparing the saplings. "We'll tell Robbie to bush-hog around them."

Jude, for her support. Though not sharing a love of writing, she allows me the time to do so. "Six hours to polish a paragraph? Why would anyone do that?"

Sir Isaac Newton, for rooting science in hope — his apple tree standing yet. From a bonk on the head, a core understanding of gravity. Though *my* trees mean nothing to the world, to me, they are anchors, inspirations; sources of wonder; seeds of dreams.

Besides, there's a benefit in the obscure. When *my* trees die, we'll not all spin off into space.

# About the Author

Neil Sampson is a horticulturist who inhabits the worlds he hears in the whisperings of abandoned apple trees. Grafting poetry with prose, he fixes the science of plant physiology with the faith typified by the seed. An historian from way back who wishes he'd stayed there, you can find Neil on Twitter: @neilsam567